SELF-HA
ISSUES

Dan Hughes

Published by
CoramBAAF Adoption and Fostering Academy
41 Brunswick Square
London WC1N 1AZ
www.corambaaf.org.uk

Coram Academy Limited, registered as a company limited by
guarantee in England and Wales number 9697712, part of the
Coram group, charity number 312278

British Library Cataloguing in Publication Data
A catalogue record for this book is available from the British Library

ISBN 978 1 913384 16 6

Project management by Jo Francis, Publications Department,
CoramBAAF
Photograph on cover from www.istockphoto.com
Designed and typeset by Fravashi Aga
Printed in Great Britain by the Lavenham Press
Trade distribution by Turnaround Publisher Services, Unit 3,
Olympia Trading Estate, Coburg Road, London N22 6TZ

 For the latest news on CoramBAAF titles and special offers, sign up
to our free publications bulletin at https://corambaaf.org.uk/subscribe.

Contents

Note about the author

For most of his professional life, **Dr Dan Hughes** has been a clinician specialising in the treatment of children and young people with severe emotional and behavioural problems. Working primarily with fostered and adopted children and their carers and parents, Dan borrowed heavily from attachment, intersubjectivity and trauma theories and research to develop a model of treatment that he calls Dyadic Developmental Psychotherapy (DDP) – also known as Attachment-Focused Family Therapy.

Dan is the author of a number of books and articles, including his previous contributions to this series: *Parenting a Child with Emotional and Behavioural Difficulties* (2012) and *Parenting a Child who has Experienced Trauma* (2016).

Dan's current passion is training therapists in his treatment model. He has trained therapists in the US, UK, Canada and other countries for the past 20 years. He also provides ongoing consultation and supervision to various agencies and clinicians. Dan has initiated a certification programme for therapists interested in his treatment model.

Dan's website: www.danielhughes.org
For information on Dyadic Developmental Psychotherapy: www.ddpnetwork.org

The series editor

Hedi Argent is an established author and editor. Her books cover a wide range of placement topics. She has written many guides and story books for young children.

Acknowledgements

I am grateful to all the readers of the manuscript for their helpful comments.

I am indebted to Jo Francis, of CoramBAAF Publications, for her unfailing good humour and support throughout our work together on this series.

Looking behind the label...

Jack has mild learning difficulties and displays some characteristics of ADHD and it is uncertain whether this will increase...

Beth and Mary have diagnoses of global developmental delay...

Abigail's birth mother has a history of substance abuse. There is no clear evidence that Abigail was prenatally exposed to drugs but her new family will have to accept developmental uncertainty...

Jade has some literacy and numeracy difficulties, but has made some improvement with the support of a learning mentor...

Prospective adopters and carers are often faced with having to decide whether they can care for a child with a health need or condition they know little about and have no direct experience of. No easy task...

Will Jack's learning difficulties become more severe?
Will Beth and Mary be able to catch up?
When will it be clear whether or not Abigail has been affected by parental substance misuse?
And will Jade need a learning mentor throughout her school life?

It can be difficult to know where to turn for reliable information. What lies behind the diagnoses and "labels" that many looked after children bring with them? And what will it be like to live with them? How will they benefit from family life?

Parenting Matters is a unique series, "inspired" by the terms used – and the need to "decode" them – in profiles of children needing new permanent families. Each title provides expert knowledge about a particular condition, coupled with facts, figures and guidance presented in a straightforward and accessible style. Each book also describes what it is like to parent an affected child, with either case studies or adopters and foster carers "telling it like it is", sharing their parenting experiences, and offering useful advice. This combination of expert information and first-hand experiences will help readers to gain understanding, and to make informed decisions.

Titles in the series deal with a wide range of health conditions and steer readers to where they can find more information. They offer a sound introduction to the topic under consideration and provide a glimpse of what it would be like to live with an affected child. Most importantly, this series looks behind the label and gives families the confidence to look more closely at a child whom they otherwise might have passed by.

Keep up with all our new books as they are published by signing up to our free publications bulletin at: https://corambaaf.org.uk/subscribe.

Titles in this series include:

- *Parenting a Child with ADHD*
- *Parenting a Child with Dyslexia*
- *Parenting a Child with Mental Health Issues*
- *Parenting a Child affected by Parental Substance Misuse*
- *Parenting a Child with Emotional and Behavioural Difficulties*
- *Parenting a Child with Autism Spectrum Disorder*
- *Parenting a Child with Developmental Delay*
- *Parenting a Child with, or at risk of, Genetic Disorders*
- *Parenting a Child affected by Domestic Violence*
- *Parenting a Child affected by Sexual Abuse*
- *Parenting a Child who has experienced Trauma*
- *Parenting a Child with Toileting Issues*
- *Parenting a Child with Eating and Food Issues*

- *Parenting a Child with Sleep Issues*
- *Parenting a Child with Difficulties in Learning caused by Trauma*

Introduction

What is self-harming behaviour in childhood?

Psychology books state that when children deliberately hurt themselves, they are engaged in self-harming behaviour. These behaviours are most often associated with a history of relational trauma, especially abuse and neglect caused by their primary caregivers. Having been subjected to extreme "punishment" by their parent, they are at risk of re-enacting these relational traumas by punishing themselves. When the parents of young children repeatedly hurt them, their children get the message: they deserve to be hurt. And too often, after a while, they take on the responsibility of hurting themselves. To them, self-harm seems right, it is how things should be. Psychology books are describing thousands of children, but often our introduction to self-harming behaviour is through our contact with one child – our foster or adopted child, a child in our classroom or our community. We need to understand this behaviour, one child at a time, and through our understanding, hopefully, support and guide that child until their sense of self is no longer experienced as deserving to be hurt.

When children have been abused (physically, sexually, emotionally) or neglected (physically, emotionally) by their primary caregivers, it is little wonder that they are at risk of self-harming behaviours. The belief that they deserve to be hurt often emerges naturally when they have been harmed by the adults they trust to keep them safe. This leads to a chronic sense of shame: 'There is something wrong with me'. Their shame will assist you – their foster carer or adoptive parent – to understand why they do things that are seen to be wrong, as well as why they are unhappy, lonely, make mistakes and hurt themselves. Your child may be living in a world where things seem hopeless and they feel helpless to change it. Self-harming behaviours may well serve as an excellent reflection of your child's inner world.

This short book is addressed to foster carers and adoptive parents who both want to understand why their child would self-harm, and more importantly, want to make a difference in their child's life so that self-harming is no longer experienced by their child as necessary, desirable, or even strangely soothing. When your child realises that you are their best source of knowledge, guidance, joy and comfort, then – and only then – will your child be able to stop self-harming behaviour.

UNDERSTANDING SELF-HARMING BEHAVIOURS

CHAPTER I

What is self-harm?

Self-harm is physical aggression against the self. The most common form is cutting oneself. Adopters and foster carers who are aware of potential self-harming behaviours will not leave dangerous objects lying about; however, children have also engaged in self-harming by hitting or scratching themselves, as well as pulling their hair out or banging their head. Some children may also poison or burn themselves or embed objects into their bodies.

If you define self-harming behaviour more broadly than physical aggression, you might include taking drugs, serious eating disorders, deliberately failing, spoiling special occasions, or engaging in behaviours meant to evoke rejection or ridicule from others. It is important to think about the possible reasons why children choose many ways to deliberately seek to hurt themselves.

Although children usually go to great lengths to hide self-harming behaviour, much too often it is seen as being "just" attention seeking or an effort to manipulate others. Believing this to be the sole or primary motive for self-harm can mean that the seriousness of the behaviour will be underestimated and the interventions used to address it will either be insufficient or make things worse. Responding negatively to self-harming behaviour, or ignoring it so as to avoid "reinforcing" it, are likely to only generate more shame in your child and thus lead to a greater likelihood that the behaviour will continue or return.

Reasons for self-harming behaviour

The following represent common reasons for self-harming behaviour. They are not mutually exclusive and they often overlap.

Self-punishment and shame

Children who hurt themselves are likely to believe that they deserve to be hurt. The actions of previous abusive parents or other caregivers only made sense to them because of what they believed to be their bad, ungrateful, selfish self. They believed that they deserved to be hurt because of who they were, not what they did. Abused and neglected children are frequently hurt when they have done nothing obviously wrong – or what they did wrong was mild, common childhood misbehaviour and did not deserve an abusive reaction.

A child's sense of being bad rapidly becomes associated with the emotion of shame because they are likely to be convinced that they are unlovable. The experience of shame is itself a very painful emotional state. Children may well hurt themselves in an effort to reduce shame through self-punishment. Self-harming behaviours in this sense may represent an effort to begin again, to start afresh. But of course, instead, it only makes the feeling of shame worse. The immediate reaction to self-harming behaviour is often, 'I'm worse than I thought, I cut myself with a knife, how sick is that?'

4

To the degree that the reason for your child's self-harming behaviour is their view of themselves as not being worthy of good care or experiences, then the interventions that address the behaviour need first to address your child's self-concept. That is more difficult than simply telling your child that they are not bad. Children – and adults – will not easily change their experience of themselves in response to lectures and reasons.

Inadequate coping skills

When children (or adults) are experiencing distress, they may develop coping skills to reduce that distress, which can often be effective (distractions, alternative behaviours, relying on someone they trust, positive self-talk, etc). But when children do not have the confidence to develop adaptive coping skills, they are at risk of engaging in coping skills that are self-harming. When children cut themselves, they may well be giving themselves specific, controllable pain to focus on, in order to take their minds off the more underlying chronic stressors of their lives. But that distraction from general stressors is very short-lived, and when the specific pain decreases, the distress is likely to return, and is often worse than ever.

An effort to take control of pain

When children are exposed to habitual abuse and neglect, they are helpless to do anything to reduce or prevent the pain they are experiencing at the hands of their caregivers. This generates a chronic state of passive hopelessness that makes the pain even more unbearable. When children themselves are the source of their own pain, it seems like a choice that they can control, although with repetition, it often becomes a habit that is hard to break. Self-harming children know, however, that the pain will be specific and short-lived, and they may well believe it to be preferable to the chronic ongoing pain coming from a source outside themselves.

Creating relief from pain

When children are able to focus on the experience of their self-harming behaviours, they are able to anticipate that the pain will end soon. It may actually feel "good" after the acute pain that they have created themselves ends. The "good" feeling is likely to be caused in part by their body's release of opioids to numb the pain and create a "high". This neurobiological response to self-induced pain makes it all the harder to reduce self-harming behaviours. (There is more about the neurobiological implications of self-harming behaviours shortly.)

An effort to "feel something"

When young children experience chronic, intense pain, they may manage to numb themselves from their emotions. Such numbing does serve as a respite from the pain, but at the cost of not feeling connected to people, events or objects. These children experience life as being empty, bleak, with little meaning or energy. When they hurt themselves, they feel acute pain, which in turn helps them to feel alive, no matter how briefly. That sense of being alive can be pleasurable when the pain is brief and able to be controlled.

An effort to inhibit aggression directed at others

When young children are placed in new families and are no longer being abused, they are both drawn into relationships with nurturing caregivers, and at the same time frightened by such relationships. Routine frustrations in their interaction with their foster carers or adoptive parents are often experienced more intensely than they would be if they did not have an abusive history. They are beginning to trust their new caregivers, and when frustrated by them, they may sense that their trust is being betrayed. By hurting themselves, they have less need to be aggressive towards their new caregivers.

An impulsive expression of their pain; an unconscious cry for help

Children with a history of abuse are likely to be exhausted by their need for constant vigilance, for suppressing their pain, and for inhibiting symptoms that make their lives more difficult. Their impulse to give expression to how difficult their life is may become so intense that they react with self-harming behaviour to release the overwhelming pressure. They may also have a fantasy that if they could only convey how hard things were for them, their compassionate caregiver would meet their needs. Parents or teachers may express shock when some children who usually seem so "normal" react to a small frustration by banging their heads against the wall.

A form of self-regulation and an effort to self-soothe

Abused and neglected children often do not trust that others will comfort them, nor do they feel that they deserve to be comforted. They believe that they have to manage their distress on their own because they cannot rely on others. They will need to experience a great deal of trust building with their new family before they begin to realise that genuine comfort, given by someone who cares for them, will reduce their pain a great deal better than their inadequate self-harming efforts. If they do not allow themselves to be cared for, the familiar experience of causing and controlling specific pain is likely to provide some sense of self-soothing relief.

The neurobiological perspective of self-harm

Just as the experience of abuse and neglect is often a daily occurence for the traumatised child, so this same child's engagement in self-harming behaviours as a coping skill may also become habitual in an effort to manage the overwhelming distress of their lives. These behavioural patterns often reflect the child's

SECTION I

neurobiological system's response to the experience of chronic trauma. An overview of the impact of relational trauma on the child's neurological development, including interventions that are based on this research, may be found in *The Neurobiology of Attachment-Focused Therapy* (Baylin and Hughes, 2016).

I asked my colleague, Jon Baylin PhD, to provide a summary for this book of these neurobiological structural and functional developments. Here is his reply (Baylin, personal communication, 2021).

Understanding the neurodynamics of self-harm starts with understanding the neurobiology of the separation distress, comfort-seeking, comfort-receiving cycle in a healthy parent–child dyad. Neuroscientists studying this process have linked it strongly to the pain system and there is now a large body of research showing that the "social pain" of separation or loss is very similar neurobiologically to physical pain. Animal studies first showed that when young mammals are separated from their mothers, they go into a state of distress associated with a decrease in opioid activity in the endorphin system. This creates a literal state of pain that triggers the separation call response in which the infant signals their distress to the caregiver whose brain responds, in kind, with a distress response that prompts the caregiver, mostly mothers, to find the young one and comfort them, return them to the nest, providing what neuroscientists call a "social buffering" effect

SECTION 1

that literally is analgesic, that turns off the distress; the social pain system enabling the young mammal to feel safe again.

When a young mammal, including a young child, does not have reliable access to a comforting adult, the infant has to adapt to this environment of harsh, unpredictable care situations. This adaptation has to start automatically, without the benefit of conscious self-defence strategies. Nature has evolved ways to provide this automatic adaptation capability. One of the important aspects of this strategy is the triggering of opioids in the young to provide analgesia and the beginnings of a self-comforting process that supports survival without having reliable, comforting relief from the pain of separation provided by a trustworthy adult.

Starting very early in life to use the automatic pain management system, that relies upon the release of opioids rather than the decrease in opioid activity that typically supports the comfort-seeking process, leads to a potentially long-term strategy of coping with a lack of trustworthy connections with other people by self-comforting, based on triggering the release of opioids to suppress pain oneself rather than relying on the comforting response of another person.

In short, what appears to be a self-harming process

is typically more connected to self-comforting, pain management, a process that gives the person control over the pain and comfort system rather than having to rely on a relational interaction.

In a sense, the child takes individual control of what would typically be under the control of a dyadic relationship. This becomes part of a multi-dimensional process of survival that shifts from a passive strategy, e.g. learned helplessness, to a more proactive strategy in which the child, and later teenager, and maybe continuing as an adult, finds a way to reduce the uncertainty of not knowing when, or if, another person is going to be comforting and helpful. By taking control of their own pain and stress management, the child is able to decrease dependency on a caregiver, literally suppressing the felt need for comfort by blocking the separation pain response system.

In a neurobiological sense, this form of self-comforting by triggering one's own opioid system is literally rewarding, and probably also triggers the dopamine system that supports learning and remembering actions, to produce further relief from pain and distress.

When we look at the abused child's self-harming behaviours from both psychological and neurobiological perspectives, we begin to see an organised pattern of behaviour meant to reduce the experience of pain inflicted by an adult, or emanating from some other deep distress without an adult available for comforting, by gaining control over self-induced physical pain that will reliably end. Such behavioural patterns may well become set, if not rigid, habits that can be difficult to change.

If you can understand your child's self-harm as a means of control, you might then consider self-harm to also be a factor in your child's behaviour that is certain to evoke a negative response from you. When this pattern develops, it is likely that your child is getting some comfort from feeling that they are controlling the negative responses that are directed at them. Such responses are experienced as being more predictable than random abuse during times when they were constantly worried that an adult would mistreat them "for no reason". There is a sense of comfort for the child in creating a predictable world in which you believe that they are bad and will respond to them with anger or criticism.

SECTION I

CHAPTER **2**

Prognosis and treatment

Prognosis

A reduction in self-harming behaviour is likely to be closely linked to your child's ability to resolve past traumatic experiences, as well as to develop a trusting relationship with you. If you focus only on the self-harming behaviour, this is likely to lead to your child feeling abnormal, stupid or bad, and will increase their resistance to whatever interventions you try. Seeing self-harming behaviours as your child's somewhat successful efforts to reduce memories of overwhelming, distressful experiences through substituting their own, is likely to normalise this coping skill and allow other, more adaptive attachment-based skills based on the relationship with you to develop.

While self-harming behaviours often reflect a history of relational trauma in childhood, they are seldom the only mental health problem associated with a history of repetitive traumas. Abuse and neglect are also associated with symptoms common in Oppositional-Defiant Disorder, Post-Traumatic Stress Disorder (PTSD), Attention Deficit Hyperactivity Disorder (ADHD), conduct disorders, dissociative disorders, anxiety and mood disorders, and early signs of personality disorders common in adulthood. All these disorders may have symptoms that range from mild to severe. The same is true of self-harming behaviours. Interventions to address self-harming behaviours need to be comprehensive, and to consider the child's functioning overall. If self-harming behaviours are to be successfully reduced, the child's mental health functioning needs to be taken into account.

As indicated in my two previous books in this series (2012, 2016), children who have experienced relational trauma and attachment insecurity or disorganisation need to live in a stable family environment to maximise their ability to resolve their traumas and to successfully address their emotional and behavioural difficulties. The same is true for children who self-harm.

Treatment

Successful treatment of children with self-harming behaviours needs to have a broad and comprehensive perspective in order to address the reasons for the behaviours' origin, while also encouraging developmental skills that will make the child's attempts to manage their distress less urgent. This perspective needs to include efforts to enhance the child's relationships with parents or caregivers, therapist, teacher, social worker, and other adults who have an influence on their development (Hughes *et al*, 2019).

Children who have experienced relational trauma, and who are therefore at greater risk of self-harming behaviour, are likely to benefit from interventions with therapeutic goals that facilitate their secure attachment to everyone who provides them with care. Research on attachment has demonstrated that three important areas of psychological development are enhanced when a child's attachment is secure (Hughes and Gurney-Smith, 2019). These are:

1. Children's ability to enter into and maintain other satisfying reciprocal relationships with important individuals in their lives. Such relationships are the source of much enjoyment and satisfaction, which further reduce the chronic experience of emotional distress that activates self-harming behaviour. The same relationships are also the source of much comfort and support, which provide the child with yet another means of reducing distress. If your child is to discover and benefit from such healing and transforming relationships, this journey will have to begin in their relationships with you – their foster carers or adoptive parents.

2. Children's ability to regulate their emotional states. The risk of self-harming behaviours increases when children experience intense emotional distress that they cannot regulate. Attachment-based therapy offers the child experiences of co-regulation of their emotional states with therapist and caregivers, which increases their ability to self-regulate.

3. Children's ability to reflect on their inner lives so that they can communicate their thoughts, feelings and wishes to others. Conversations about their inner life are likely to increase their readiness to understand and accept troubling experiences, to reduce their sense of shame, and to share with safe attachment figures their level of distress and the support they need.

Therapy for your child who self-harms therefore needs to focus on your child's overall life story. We have come to understand the importance of writing a child's life story for and with them, so that they may develop an understanding of the many events in their life. This story certainly needs to include information about parents, siblings and other caregivers, as well as places and events that have been significant for the child. When a child has experienced abuse and/or neglect, those events also need to be presented in enough detail to enable the child to organise the experiences that have had such a big influence on their life. When young children are abused and neglected, they strive to make sense of what happened and why. Invariably, young children will develop a story that includes a belief that they are bad and/or unlovable and deserve to be punished. They are also likely to experience these events as having been impossible to avoid, the situation being hopeless to change, and being helpless under the control of abusers. The overriding goal of therapy is to help the child to develop a new understanding about remembered abusive events. These new meanings help the child to understand that while they experienced the events as being their fault, they were, in fact, due to the betrayals, failures and hurtful behaviours of adults who should have given care and comfort.

If therapy is successful in helping your child to develop an integrative story that goes beyond the experiences of shame and fear that characterise the original story, then there is an increased possibility for your child to regard self-harming behaviours as not fitting who they are beginning to think they are. In the new story, your child may well be starting to experience the relationships with you, the caregivers, as the source of comfort and joy, which is so much more effective in dealing with distress than specific pain-inducing self-harm. As the story changes, so the meaning and value of self-harming behaviour also changes. The child's sense of who they are changes, and as a sense of self-worth increases, the need for self-punishment decreases.

Here is a brief vignette of how this therapeutic process is likely to occur.

CASE STUDY

Kevin is talking with a therapist. He is 10 years old and has been in foster care for three years following seven years during which he experienced considerable physical abuse as well as neglect while living with his birth parents. Kevin's foster carers are present.

The therapist has been able to establish the conversational tone of the therapeutic dialogue to increase Kevin's readiness and ability to have a conversation about any and all aspects of his life. In most sessions, the conversation begins with a focus on light, interesting and safe themes and then – without changing vocal tone or intensity – blends into dialogue about the more stressful experiences of the past and/or present.

Therapist: So why did you think that your dad was abusing you?

Kevin: I was a bad kid! He wouldn't have abused me if I wasn't bad!

Therapist: Oh, I understand now what you think about what happened! You think that your dad hurt you because you were bad. That must have been extra hard for you then, both being hurt and also thinking that you're a bad boy!

Kevin: Well, I was…and still am!

Therapist: Oh! And you still think that you're bad! All this time you've been thinking that your life has been so hard – because you deserve it!

Kevin: I do!

Therapist: Ah! Now I understand better why you hit
             yourself on the side of your head, and scratch
             and bite yourself, when you're upset. Seems
             like you feel that you should punish yourself if
             something goes wrong. Like it's your fault, so
             you should hurt yourself.

Kevin: (*much quieter*) I guess. I know it's not Kim or
             Jim's (*foster carers*) fault. They're not being mean
             to me.

Therapist: Ah! Even if your parents hurt you – were mean
             to you – you know that your foster carers
             don't do that…so you must be to blame…
             you're the bad one!

Kevin: I am.

Therapist: I wonder, Kevin, if when Kim or Jim say 'no' to
             you…sometimes you do think that they're not
             being fair…that they are hurting you just like
             your parents did. And if they are hurting you,
             maybe you think it's because they think that
             you're bad, just like your parents did.

Kevin: Yeah. They don't call me bad. They're not
             supposed to. But they think it.

Therapist: Ah! Kevin! How hard things still are for you.
             It seems to you that your foster carers think
             that you're bad. So you should hurt yourself.
             Like this has been happening all your life and it
             probably seems like it will never change.

Kevin: It won't.

Therapist: Have you told your foster carers that, Kevin?
             Have you told them that it seems to you that
             they think you're bad and they're right?

Kevin: No.

Therapist: Would you tell them? I'd like to know what they'll say.

Kevin: (to Kim and Jim) You do think that I'm bad. (tearfully)

Kim: Oh, Kevin, that must be hard if you think that! No wonder you get so upset when we say 'no' to you. You think it means that we are being mean to you because we think you're bad.

Kevin: Don't you?

Kim: I don't think you're bad, Kevin. But you do, and that is more important than what I think now. I hope someday you'll agree that what I think about you – you're a good kid who makes some mistakes and tries really hard to figure out how to have a good life – might be who you actually are. That maybe who you are is closer to what Jim and I think about you, not what your parents thought about you.

Therapist: What do you think about what Kim said, Kevin?

Kevin: I don't know…I don't know.

Such conversations will encourage your child to reflect on their life and, hopefully, to have doubts about their negative feelings about themselves that they developed while living with primary carers who abused and neglected them. From such doubts, a new sense of self may emerge, followed by a reduction in self-harming behaviours.

Having access to the right kind of therapy can be difficult and require determination, perseverance, and a social worker on your side.

CHAPTER 3

Frequently asked questions

This chapter sets out clear, practical answers to a number of frequently asked, day-to-day questions about children's self-harming behaviours.

Is it best to ignore self-harming behaviour so as not to reinforce it?

When the intention of a child's specific behaviour is to evoke a particular response from another person, and when that person does respond in this way, it is more likely that the behaviour will be repeated (it will be reinforced). However, the intention of the child's self-harming behaviour is to manage their own overwhelming emotional distress and to experience some relief from their negative feelings of self-worth. These factors are independent of the adult's reinforcing reactions. Therefore, ignoring self-harming behaviour may be experienced by your child as indifference to their distress and safety.

If the natural consequence of self-harming behaviour is pain, why does that not cause the behaviour to stop?

If the only consequence of self-harming was pain, then the behaviour might well stop. However, there are many other consequences, with more positive qualities for children who self-harm than the negative quality of pain. These include exerting control over their emotions, distracting themselves from their experience of chronic distress, validating their sense of worthlessness, and providing an escape from their deep-rooted defensive position of not feeling anything.

When my child hurts themself, I feel that it must be my fault. How do I stop blaming myself?

Children's self-harming behaviour reflects their own sense of shame and hopelessness. Knowing this, you would, of course, experience empathy for your child and so feel some of their pain. It is important to reflect on your child's past history of abuse and neglect in order to remind yourself that the self-harming tendencies are rooted in relationships that preceded their relationship with you. Reflect too, on the positive experiences you have provided for your child, which will hopefully, in time, reduce the factors that have led to habits of self-harm.

My child knows that I will not blame them when they feel like hurting themself. Why don't they just talk to me about it so I can help?

Your child is likely to be ambivalent about self-harming because of the many factors that caused that behaviour in the first place, and might not always want your help. Also, self-harm is a means of exerting control over pervasive negative emotional states and your child is likely to be reluctant to give that control over to you. The feeling of shame is likely to cause them to justify hurting themselves. Finally, it is difficult for children to reflect on the factors that lead to self-harm, so they will probably have problems in communicating them to you.

My child knows how scared they were when their parents hurt them, so why do they still do to themselves what their parents did to them?

When children are hurt by their parents, the experience is made worse by not having any control over what is happening. There is a tendency after such an experience to re-enact the event, this time being in control of the situation in an effort to resolve it. A second reason involves the *meaning* that the children take away from being hurt by their parents. Most often they interpret the abuse as being a sign that they are bad and deserve to be hurt. By hurting themselves, they are essentially agreeing with their parents and punishing themselves for being bad. Young children are not able to realise that it is their parents, and not they, who are wrong and to blame.

My child has so many opportunities to behave in ways that would make them happy and proud. Why do they still engage in behaviours that have the opposite effect?

Regretfully, when children develop a self-image of being bad, they tend to be comfortable with whatever validates their negative sense of self, and uncomfortable with anything that conflicts with their negative concept. Abused and neglected children are often very uncomfortable with positive feedback and misbehave straight after being praised. This is "negative attention-seeking", which in some ways is a psychological expression of self-harming behaviour.

Is self-harming behaviour an early stage of suicidal behaviour?

No. The great majority of children who self-harm do not engage in suicidal behaviour. Having said that, it is true that among the much smaller number of children who show suicidal tendencies, many have also self-harmed. While self-harming and suicidal behaviours are seen as separate conditions, they are both generally preceded by extreme negative experiences over a lengthy period of time, and consequently a very negative sense of self. When a child is self-harming, it usually does not mean that they require continuous supervision or hospitalisation, which might well be necessary when a child is suicidal.

CHAPTER 4

How your child might be affected at different stages of development

As is the case with most symptoms, self-harming behaviour is likely to be expressed differently depending upon your child's chronological age and/or developmental level. It is wise to remember that many looked after and adopted children may be operating at a lower developmental age than might be suggested by their chronological age.

Children aged two–five

For the two–five-year-old child, self-harming behaviours often represent the young child's pervasive, overwhelming sense of terror or ongoing intense anxiety about the moment-to-moment experiences in their life. Their regulation and reflective skills have only begun to develop, and if they are not receiving the support that they need for these important developmental tasks, then their extreme behavioural reaction to the situation might easily cause the young child great harm, although it may well not be "intentional".

An attachment relationship is crucial to help children in this age range to manage the overwhelming feelings associated with the immediate event. When a child is psychologically and physically alone in the face of terror, they may well be experiencing a sense of annihilation. The self is shattered by the external trauma.

Children aged six–twelve

For the six–twelve-year-old child, the traumatic events that activated self-harming tendencies – being hurt by their parents during their early years – are more recent than they would be for an adolescent who was adopted at a young age. Therefore competing safety-enhancing, nurturing experiences with their new family are not perceived as often or as strongly as they might be later, after more years in this environment.

If the child's sense of shame and their habitual mistrust of others are still dominant, then the risk of self-harming will be greater.

Pre-adolescence

In pre-adolescence (commonly described as being from age ten to age thirteen), self-harm is often an impulsive reaction to an immediate source of distress. The child's ability to inhibit such impulses is not as great as it is likely to be in later adolescence. Behaviours are not planned as much as they are a reaction to the intense emotion of the moment.

Adolescence

As children enter adolescence, they develop a greater ability to reflect on their experiences of self and become more capable of developing another story about their self that differs from the original punitive, abusive version. Also, their ability to inhibit their impulses will be stronger, and cognitive strategies to manage self-harming will be greater. These enhanced reflective and regulatory skills in later adolescence may well reduce some of the risk of self-harming.

However, at the same time, an adolescent is more likely than a younger child to plan self-harming behaviour in order to make it more effective. Planning will help the young person to regulate their negative emotional states, as well as making it less likely that they will be caught while self-harming. Knowing that they have a plan to successfully self-harm may reduce the need to impulsively hurt themselves in the moment. Self-harming behaviour may become more gratifying through neurological repetition of the behaviour, and also, adolescents are more able to sufficiently delay gratification so that the self-harming behaviour is more effective. Self-harming behaviour may release dopamine which brings pleasure to the act, and with repetition, anticipatory dopamine is likely to create a desire to self-harm rather than an avoidance of any actual harm. With delay of immediate gratification, the adolescent may feel in control of a situation, believing that they can create the desired effect in the future, whenever they choose to do so. This reduces the sense of helplessness that they most often feel.

SECTION I

25

CHAPTER **5**

Educational and social issues

The traumatised child is likely to have more difficulty managing educational and social expectations than is the child who has not experienced relational trauma in their early childhood. These situations are likely to create more pervasive anxiety, greater shame and doubt, and more realistic failures than the challenges of life at home. Relational trauma places at risk children's social, emotional and cognitive developmental skills that are important in managing the academic and peer expectations that they will face outside the home.

Educational issues

The child's teacher will certainly hold academic expectations that may well be challenging for the child to achieve. The traumatised child is at risk of having learning difficulties and attention span and concentration problems because so much of their brain is caught up in coping with the emotional distress that is causing them to self-harm (Hurley, 2021). This, along with impulsivity and a need for immediate gratification, may compromise the child's school performance. Because the teacher is unlikely to know the child as well as their foster carers or adoptive parents do, it will be harder for the teacher to match the full range of academic, social and emotional expectations with the child's ability, especially since such abilities are likely to vary from day to day depending on the child's sense of safety and varying, competing motivations.

With your child's knowledge and consent, it is wise to inform their teacher, without going into details, that your child experienced many stressful and even traumatic events when younger that may well affect them academically, as well as their psychological and social functioning. Suggest to the teacher that patience and understanding are needed when expectations are made about your child's behaviour. Also, indicate that your child's sense of safety may be easily disturbed, and that when not feeling safe, your child's behaviour is likely to deteriorate. Stress that you are interested in your child's total well-being, not solely their academic performance, and that you would like to maintain open communication about all aspects of their functioning at school. It might be wise to express your concerns about the challenges your child faces in general, without referring to any self-harming behaviours. Being alerted to self-harming behaviours could result in teachers becoming too vigilant and giving a child an uncomfortable sense of being watched all the time, or teachers may interpret your concerns as suggesting that your child might be suicidal.

Social issues

Children's peers will also generally not be as sensitive to a child's particular skills and challenges as their foster carers or adoptive parents are. As cannot be stated too often, the foundation of a child's success in their foster or adoptive home will depend on their sense of acceptance within this new family. Foster carers and adoptive parents will hopefully see that their child's behaviour stems from their damaged sense of self, and restrict their evaluations to the child's behaviour, while striving to enhance the child's sense of self. Peers are usually less ready and able to do that. They are also likely to have expectations based on chronological rather than developmental age – and as mentioned previously, these may well be very different in looked after and adopted children.

Your child may need guidance from you about the challenges that they are likely to face in relationships with peers outside the home who do not understand the impact of traumatic experiences. You might suggest that while talking to peers about their early history could create a positive response, it is possible that some peers will avoid them if they know their history. Your child may benefit from your empathy about the difficulties of relating to peers in general, and especially when there is a risk of not feeling safe in response to conflicts or being mistreated. Responding with PACE (Playfulness, Acceptance, Curiosity and Empathy; see Chapter 6) when your child does express distress relating to peer difficulties is likely to be the best first response. Depending on the situation, you might be required to take a more active, supportive role, providing advocacy and advice to your child and others.

The importance of attachment

When your child returns home from school or social settings, be attentive to their emotional state and help them to become more reflective and regulated if necessary. Your child may especially need to develop the sense that home can be a sanctuary away from the stresses of daily life. It is therefore all the more important that your child has developed a secure attachment to you. This will enable them to rely on you for comfort, to co-regulate their emotional state with you, and to reflect with you about daily events in a manner that reduces their associations with shame and fear.

Finally, a secure attachment will enable your child to discover how to interact with you in a manner that creates mutual delight and enjoyment. Until your child is able to develop these psychological and emotional skills in relation to their attachment figures, they will not be able to benefit as much as you would hope from your encouragement and advice regarding academic and social challenges.

SECTION 1

CHAPTER **6**

Specific parenting tasks

There are a number of specific parenting tasks that you can concentrate on when trying to help your child with their self-harming behaviours.

Establish an ongoing sense of safety

It is important for a carer or parent to keep in mind that a child's sense of safety is crucial if they are to develop the relational, regulatory and reflective skills needed to have positive expectations about life and a sense of their worth and abilities. For safety to exist for the child, it is important that:

- they are able to trust that their basic psychological and physical needs will be met;

- their daily life is predictable, enabling them to be

confident that trauma will be avoided;

- they know that they are safely held in the minds and hearts of their new parents or carers, who do not forget them and whose love is unconditional;

- they are able to rely on their parents or carers for the guidance and support they need to manage challenges and stress.

Relate with PACE (Playful, Accepting, Curious, Empathic)

Children who have experienced maltreatment and neglect often have great difficulty understanding and expressing qualities of their inner life. They are likely to be unaware of what they think, feel or want. As a result, they often react to situations without an understanding of why they did what they did, or of what they need to do to ensure better results in the future.

The child who is at risk of self-harming is likely to have a core assumption that their life is hopeless, that they are unable to make it any better, and that therefore the future holds out no promise of improvement.

Parents and carers need to stand alongside their non-reflective children to provide them with the skills to become increasingly aware of their inner life. The child will then be able to develop adaptive and reflective coping skills to deal with the challenges ahead, rather than relying on the narrow range of self-destructive survival skills that are rooted in their abusive past.

PACE is an attitude and way of being with your child that gives priority to understanding and responding to your child's inner life prior to, and in addition to, your response to their behaviours. It is

31

your attitude when interacting with your child that facilitates your child's attachment to you (Golding and Hughes, 2012), and it is this attitude that is central to the practice of Dyadic Developmental Psychotherapy (DDP) (Hughes *et al*, 2019). Too often during the day-to-day challenges of raising your child, especially a child with disturbing behaviours, you are likely to react by focusing on "managing" the behaviours: by evaluating and correcting, all in the interest of teaching your child appropriate social skills to ensure that they will develop into a successful and co-operative member of your family and community. While that is a necessary task of parenting, often our guide about what, and how, we teach our child is based on our assumptions about the meaning of their behaviour. PACE helps parents and carers to slow down and make sense of their child's behaviours before deciding how to interact with the child in regard to these behaviours.

Playfulness

Playfulness is an often-overlooked way of engaging with a traumatised child. We may be so aware of the child's past traumas and their present challenging behaviours that we forget that healthy families enjoy playfulness as a normal part of daily life. Playfulness is an important element in helping a child begin to thrive and to make the most of the opportunities provided in a healthy family.

Playfulness conveys delight, enjoyment and acceptance of the here-and-now, highlights the sense that the relationship between child and parent/carer is "for better or worse" and that much satisfaction within the family comes from spontaneous activities involving being together, enjoying each other's companionship, rather than through teaching or achieving. Playfulness ensures that your child will know why you are striving to help them to learn how to do better. Playfulness is often the background, the position from which love is experienced and communicated.

CASE EXAMPLE – PLAYFULNESS

An 11-year-old boy said that his foster carer *always* said 'no' when he asked to be allowed to do something. The foster carer seemed confused when she heard him say that, and was then thoughtful, and finally said that she recalled saying 'no' only three times the day before at most, whereas she recalled saying 'yes' at least five times the same day.

Sure enough, over the next five days, she noted that she did only say 'no' three times or less each day, and said 'yes' over five times. She gently pointed this out to the child and asked for an apology. Over the course of the next day, the boy asked her if he could do, or have, quite a number of things that she had to say 'no' to. These included requests for her to buy him a new bike, allow him to eat cookies before supper, and play a video game rather than doing his homework. At the fifth 'no', he could not hide his grin, and she realised that he was trying to prove her wrong. 'That's not fair!' she yelled, and she chased him around the house while he kept making increasingly outrageous requests. They ended up in fits of laughter together.

Acceptance

Acceptance follows closely on from playfulness to convey the unconditional quality of the parental relationship and the meaning of "family". Acceptance, when actively communicated, helps a child to truly experience that you are only evaluating, criticising, or angry, with their behaviour, but not with the child themselves or your relationship with them. The relationship is always more important than the particular conflict, and when your child trusts your commitment to the relationship is secure, they are more likely to be able to listen to your evaluation of their behaviour without becoming defensive and oppositional.

Actively communicating acceptance of your child is crucial if you hope to reduce your child's sense of shame, which is so often central in self-harming behaviours. Pervasive shame causes children to believe that they deserve to be punished because they are inherently bad and/or unlovable and therefore worthless. They believe that they deserve the stressful or punitive treatments they have received, and will receive again. When they make a mistake or do something wrong, they interpret that as a reflection of their bad self, not simply as common, childish misbehaviour. They are convinced that the problem is not that they *did* something wrong, but rather that they *are* stupid, selfish or lazy, and deficient in their core being. Whereas a poor choice is something that one can change and learn from, self-deficiency is likely to seem impossible to change.

Helping a child with their sense of shame is more difficult than one might think. Since the child is convinced that they are bad, if you tell them that they are wrong, that they are not bad, you will not be believed. Rather, they may think that you simply do not know how bad they are, or that you are lying out of a sense of duty. They may also think that they have successfully manipulated you and that you will eventually see through their deceptions.

If you disagree with your child over their sense of shame, their bad behaviour is likely to get worse since they will feel that they cannot trust your views and will probably work hard to negate them. Children like this are motivated to protect their sense of self, even when it is based on shame. If you are to influence your child's behaviour, your ability to influence their sense of self will need to come first.

You are most likely to help your child with their sense of shame by:

- communicating an understanding about your child's experience: 'It seems that because of what you did, you think that you're just bad'.

- expressing empathy for their sense of shame: 'It must be hard for you to think that you are bad whenever you do something wrong'.

- being curious about, and so helping your child to be curious about, their shame: 'Are there times when you don't think you're bad when you've done something wrong?', or: 'How long do you think you've felt that way about yourself?', or: 'How do you handle those feelings? Because they must be hard.'

These responses will emphasise your acceptance and help your child to be aware of, reflect on, and hopefully begin to question and doubt their experiences of shame.

Curiosity

Curiosity can be seen as an important part of your attitude toward your child when you want them to become more aware of their inner life, and when you want to understand their behaviour and so respond to it in the most helpful manner. Curiosity needs to be a non-judgemental stance for you to take towards your child's thoughts, feelings, wishes, perceptions, judgements and memories; qualities of your child's inner life seen as simply being what they are, not being right or wrong. If you evaluate or judge your child's inner life, they will be less likely to explore it and share their views with you. Many adolescents do not talk with their parents about their inner life at all because their parents have suggested that they should not think, feel or want something or other. When you focus on understanding your child's inner life, they are much more likely to become engaged with you in understanding it too. If you say, 'Why did you do that?' in a judgemental, harsh tone, your child is likely to become defensive and non-communicative. If you say, 'I wonder why you did that?' with total openness and acceptance conveyed in your tone, your child is more likely to wonder along with you, and to share their emerging thoughts.

Curiosity is a "not-knowing" stance, without assumptions about the meaning of your child's inner life. Assumptions reduce the openness to possible meanings and tend to increase defensiveness. A "not-knowing" real curiosity is non-evaluative. It demonstrates a desire to understand, not judge, and to uncover the meaning of behaviour. A curious attitude will reduce your child's defensiveness and increase their motivation to understand why they do what they do. Because of their long-term pervasive feelings of shame, they may often assume that whatever motives led to their behaviour must be wrong, since they are wrong. So they do not wonder about why they do what they do, what they think and feel, or who they are. Those questions are too painful when the child is overcome by shame. By helping your child to begin to wonder along with you about their inner life, they may begin to see other possibilities that do not involve being bad or worthless.

Empathy

Empathy enables your child to explore, address and, finally, to face the difficult areas of their life – both their past traumas, but also their current misbehaviours – without having to engage in the process alone. Empathy conveys that you understand that the reasons for their challenging behaviours are rooted in their terrifying memories, and that you are giving them the support and confidence to sustain them, as they attempt to understand their past and present.

Empathy is an affective, bodily response to the distress experienced by another person. It communicates that I "get" your experience and I am with you in it, experiencing it with you. It is activated by distress. If your child is engaged in self-harming behaviour, they are unlikely to be giving direct expression to their distress, thus making it harder for you to empathise with them. What you need to do is to actively recall your child's traumatic history. This will enable you to feel compassion, and when your child experiences your compassion, they are likely to reveal some vulnerability which, in turn, will enable you to show empathy towards them. At that point, your child is not alone with their trauma. We are all able to experience, make sense of, and resolve trauma more successfully when someone we trust is with us in a joint effort to comprehend our traumatic experience.

Understand and express empathy for your child's distress. Empathy, much more than reassurance, information or reasoning, is likely to enable your child to regulate their experience of distrust. Your child's need to self-regulate through self-harming behaviours is then likely to become lessened. The tendency to relate and attach to others who can and will co-regulate the distress, with empathy, is then likely to increase.

SECTION I

CHAPTER **7**

Addressing self-harming behaviour as it happens

Most likely, you are feeling a need for ideas about how to respond *in the moment* when your child is engaging in self-harming behaviours. It is very common for parents and carers to not know what to do at these times. The following suggestions might be of value.

- Remain emotionally regulated. Do not get agitated or angry.

- Check to see if any medical intervention is needed when your child self-harms. If you think urgent attention is required, do not hesitate to call an ambulance or access necessary medical help.

- While expressing empathy for your child's distress, direct them to stop immediate self-harming behaviour.

- If your words cannot stop your child's self-harming

behaviour, then intervene physically and get help if necessary.

- If you are not agitated or angry, engage your child in a conversation about what is happening for them at this moment. Remember PACE in your reaction (see previous chapter).

- If your child needs time/space before being able to engage with you, and is not in danger, give them however much time/space is needed.

- Adopt a non-judgemental attitude of wanting to understand what is happening in your child's mind.

- Don't argue with expressions of shame from your child. Try instead to generate a more positive view of your child's sense of self through your empathy and curiosity.

- Offer comfort to your child through your non-verbal and verbal expressions.

- Wonder if your child would like you to help explore ways to prevent them from trying to hurt themself in the future. Suggest to them that if not now, perhaps they will let you know if they change their mind later. When they are open to your ideas, have some in the back of your mind that might fit your child, such as engaging in distracting or competitive activities, signalling to you when they need help, or staying close to you.

To focus now on what you might think of as a more general, long-term approach to meeting the needs of a child who is self-harming: it all begins with safety. Through giving your child a sense of safety, by exploring and understanding their inner life, by relating to them with PACE, you are providing your child with an environment that will make them more able to address their self-harming behaviours. Keep the following in mind.

39

Anticipate

First of all, you need to be aware of situations that are likely to be stressful for your child because they are frightening, rejecting, or reminders of past traumas. You need to be aware of your child's specific "triggers", most likely connected to their history, that might activate a tendency to self-harm. It is important not to forget that what seems to you like a positive event may make your child anxious, which, in turn, might activate self-harming behaviours. Successes, praise or signs of affection might cause children to feel that they do not deserve such experiences and that they must punish themselves. The act of self-punishment might also help a child to regulate the emotion aroused by the positive event.

If you anticipate that positive experiences might evoke anxieties in your child that could activate self-harming behaviour, please do not avoid exposing your child to positive experiences. However, it might be wise not to "sing their praises" for all to hear, as that might cause them to feel acute anxiety. Acknowledge something your child might be proud of without judging it to be all-important. Enjoy any success together, without judgemental praise. Remember that for a sense of safety, the experience of acceptance is much more valuable than particular positive evaluations. If you see that your child might be experiencing anxiety associated with success, always respond with acceptance, curiosity and empathy, and take your cue from them as to what they need from you at that moment.

Notice

Look for changes in your child's behaviour that might reflect intense distress, such as agitation, withdrawal, irritability, self-criticism, being secretive, efforts to deny stressful events, or anything else worrisome. Are there signs of self-harm in their clothing, skin or face? (Some children will regularly hide marks of self-harm under long-sleeved clothes, even in hot weather.)

Understand

Understand your child's self-harming behaviours rather than evaluating or trying to stop them. Most evaluations are likely to create defensiveness about what your child did due to feelings of shame or anxiety. Your child is then likely to become more secretive about their self-harming. If you are curious about self-harming without judgement, your child will probably be more open about it and they may then reflect on self-harming in a way that will lead to a much deeper understanding of it.

When your child does not feel judged regarding their behaviours, they are more likely to develop a greater awareness of them. This might be the opening you need to have your child work with you, rather than oppose you, in efforts to establish control over self-harming. When your child is motivated (and not before), then making plans to ask for help, to engage in alternative behaviours, to explore ways in which you may comfort them and they might soothe themselves appropriately, are more likely to be successful.

Discover, share and accept your child's emerging sense of self-worth

Helping your child to accept and value themselves is much more likely to result in a reduction of self-harming behaviours than focusing on trying to limit those behaviours through increased supervision, structure, information or rewards. If children truly "like" themselves, they are much less likely to feel a need to punish themselves and are more likely to question and inhibit any self-harming tendencies. Your abused child is likely to have a damaged sense of self that activates self-harming behaviours. As this sense of self is gradually replaced by a sense of self that is acceptable, worthy, and cherished by self and others, then there will be little motivation for self-harming behaviours.

To help your child to develop a more positive sense of self-worth is not as easy as we would like it to be. Self-worth does not come from proof, reason or information. Certainly, arguing with your child to prove that they are not bad will have little effect. If anything, such arguments will cause a child to feel more isolated, sensing that you truly do not know them as they "really" are. However, you are able to help your child on a journey of increased self-worth in a gradual manner, through daily living and joint experiences, rather than through rational teaching. This journey is likely to contain the following.

- The features of PACE in your relationship with your child, as described above and in the previous chapter. PACE differentiates self from behaviour so that your child experiences your unconditional acceptance of their self, even if you have to limit their behaviour.

- Empathy, in particular, is likely to help your child to feel vulnerable regarding the abusive events in their life, followed by compassion for self. Empathy conveys, not through reason, but through being connected with a caring adult in the painful memory of abuse, that they did not deserve to be hurt.

- As your child begins to discover new traits about their self, you will discover them too and be able to celebrate and feel joy together. Your deepening experiences of your child's strengths will help them to recognise these qualities in themselves.

- This joint discovery of these emergent strengths and positive qualities is not the same as praise. Praise is a judgement that is likely to make your child uncomfortable and your words unbelievable. However, joint positive experiences may also cause your child to be anxious, since they contradict their old sense of self, and may lead to feelings of uncertainty as to who they really are. Empathy may well then have to alternate with the delight and joy over jointly discovered self-worth.

- Express and model comfort and support towards all members of the family. Just as others deserve to be comforted, so does your adopted or fostered child. Acknowledge your own mistakes and hard times – you are not perfect either, but you do not deserve to be punished. Accept the positive and negative events of daily life as simply being a natural part of life's uncertainties. We do not deserve to be punished when we get it wrong.

- Celebrate and highlight activities that clearly include your child as a valued family member who contributes to it just as do the other family members; who has a part in family rituals and gatherings; who has their own unique contribution to make to your family that cannot be made by anyone else.

SECTION I

SECTION I

Conclusion

Self-harming behaviour by fostered and adopted children may best be understood as one of many possible expressions of the impact of abuse or neglect on a young child. In ideal or "good enough" homes, young children develop strong attachment behaviours, which enables them to turn to their parents or carers for safety and self-discovery. They trust their parents or carers with their physical and psychological development. When parents or other primary carers abuse and neglect their children, they are betraying their trust by teaching them lies about their worth and the nature of relationships – lies that they are bad and that they need to mistrust the adults in their lives. This betrayal generates pervasive mistrust that impacts on children's future relationships with caregivers, teachers, social workers and peers, while also making it hard for the young child to learn how to regulate their emotional states, reflect on the meaning of events in their life, and trust that they deserve, and will receive, good care. Self-harming behaviours reflect all of these consequences of early trauma.

In helping your child to control their self-harming behaviours, you will be helping them to re-experience their sense of self so that they discover that they are worthy of good care and deserve your protection. As they learn to regulate their emotional states, they become more able to inhibit tendencies to self-harm. As they reflect on their old life story in contrast with the new one that is developing in your home, they are learning that there is no place for pervasive shame in their sense of self, and no need to try to self-soothe or to control their life through creating specific, limited sources of pain by hurting their own bodies. They are learning how to rely on your care, to discover themselves in your eyes and mind, and to partake in the joint family experiences that will together enable them to manage the routine stressors of their daily life. Then they will be able not just to inhibit self-harming behaviours, but also to give expression to self-enhancing thoughts, emotions and behaviour.

SECTION 1

PARENTING CHILDREN AFFECTED BY SELF-HARMING BEHAVIOURS

Nine-year-old Ben shouts out: 'They're not mean!'

Ben's story

Ben was a nine-year-old-boy, who had been living with his adoptive parents, Kate and Taylor, for the past two years. He came into foster care when he was five, after living with his mother since birth. During his first five years, Ben was physically abused by his mother and by two men she had a relationship with. He also experienced ongoing physical and emotional neglect. Ben's mother originally made marginal efforts to reunite with Ben when he was taken into foster care, but made no effort to address the issues in her life that put her son at risk, and she eventually lost interest in having any regular contact with him.

Between the ages of five and seven, Ben lived in three different foster homes. His behaviour was very challenging, characterised by explosive outbursts if he was restrained, great difficulty in accepting responsibility for the consequences of his actions, and by being seemingly indifferent to the possibility of seeking a closer relationship with his foster carers. He lied a great deal and seldom spoke about his thoughts, feelings or wishes. His foster carers often said, 'He just doesn't care!' He was also challenging at school. Along with emotional outbursts, he had difficulty attending to his studies and was oppositional with his teachers. He had many conflicts with his peers. The foster carers in his third foster home agreed to keep Ben until an adoptive home was found for him.

His adoption social worker, Emmy, found Ben to be both engaging and confusing; ready to chat with her about everything during one visit, and ignoring her the next. She never knew quite how he would respond if she praised him, expressed interest in what he was doing, or offered him support. She gradually took a more receptive attitude towards him, allowing him to initiate interactions and requests rather than taking the lead. In this way, she hoped that he would feel in control of the relationship, something that seemed to be important to him.

When Ben was first placed with his adoptive parents, his behaviour was quite similar to how it had been in his foster homes. Kate and Taylor had anticipated this, but they were committed to making the placement work. They were content with the likelihood that progress would be slow. He was their son – for better or worse.

Kate and Taylor joined an adoption programme

that focused more on establishing relationships with traumatised children and less on behaviour management. They were given training in relating with PACE, which helped them to see the signs that their adopted child did not trust them. They realised that they had to build trust before Ben could begin to rely on them. They were encouraged to develop the habit of trying to understand what Ben's behaviour meant, before deciding how to respond to the behaviour. They quickly discovered that they often had to ask each other, 'What does it mean?' in response to Ben's unpredictable behaviours. When they asked Ben why he did something, he would invariably say, 'I don't know'. They gradually realised that most of the time this was true. Ben really did not know why he did things, just as he often did not know what he thought or felt or wanted.

Kate and Taylor turned to Emmy, Ben's adoption social worker, for support and ideas. She helped them to realise that in caring for Ben, they could be at risk of experiencing "blocked care". Blocked care involves a developing parental attitude that results in the parent or carer continuing to meet their child's basic needs, while the enjoyment, interest and meaning in the interactions with their child are hard to maintain. This state is likely to result from trying to care for a child who consistently rejects your care. That was the case with Ben. Not only did he become angry with Kate and Taylor's routine expectations and limits, he also habitually refused their efforts to provide him with support, comfort and guidance. At times, he seemed to enjoy being with them, to initiate activities with them and even to talk about things that were on his mind. But these times were short-lived, and tended to lead toward an increase in irritable, oppositional behaviour. Ben did not seem to trust having "good times" together, and whenever he happened to get closer to Kate and Taylor, and became aware of it, he was certain to push them away again. Because these periods of Ben becoming engaged with them were so short, it caused Kate and Taylor to eventually doubt how genuine he was. Was he simply being manipulative? Still, it was better than never having any "good times" together, and it helped them somewhat to remain committed to trying to reach their son.

Kate and Taylor also worried about how often Ben seemed to get hurt. He would play outside and invariably come in covered in scratches and bruises. If they wanted to take care of him, he would become annoyed and say that small bruises did not bother him. At times, it even seemed like he deliberately hurt himself. How else could he cut himself with a fork? Or cause a severe bruise on his leg from simply bumping against the table? When they asked him about these incidents, Ben just became angry and walked away. Kate and Taylor became increasingly confused about Ben and uncertain about how best to relate to him. One day, an event occurred that led them to request an urgent meeting with Emmy.

A concerning incident

Kate told Emmy that two days earlier, they had taken Ben to a nearby lake for a swim and lunch. They thought that Ben was having a good time, he had learned to swim quickly and he loved it! He complained about having to leave, but transitions were always hard for him, and his annoyance did not seem to be unusually intense. But he still seemed agitated when they returned home, and to help him to "get out his energy", they suggested that he play in the back garden. A bit later, Taylor looked for Ben from the kitchen window and saw him standing next to a big tree in their garden, banging his head hard against it. They ran outside to stop him. By the time they got close to him, Ben had stopped banging his head but his forehead was bleeding. Before they could say anything, he yelled that he had fallen out of the tree. When Taylor challenged him and said that he saw him banging his head, Ben screamed that Taylor was lying and then ran into the house. Kate and Taylor followed him, but he refused to talk to them, and only allowed Kate to clean his cut after Taylor left the room. He still would not talk about what had happened.

Kate and Taylor told Emmy that they had never seen Ben hurt himself like that before, although he often had cuts or bruises after playing outside. He would always say that he had fallen or bumped into something while running. They had no idea as to why he had banged his head against the tree. They said that it was often hard to tell why he got upset about things. It was hard to predict what his moment-to-moment emotional state would be.

Emmy reviewed other areas of Ben's life, such as school and peer relationships. She also asked if Kate and Taylor ever had regrets over having adopted him. She was relieved when they said that their commitment to him was as strong as ever. Emmy said that she would come back and speak with Ben the next day. She needed some time to think about how to approach Ben in order to create the best opportunity for him to talk to her. She needed to help Ben – as well as Kate and Taylor. Ben was a vulnerable child who would be further traumatised if the adoption became unstable.

Emmy arrived the next day to see Ben riding his bike in the front driveway. She had to be careful as she approached the house because he darted back and forth in front of her car. Ben showed little interest in talking to her, so she went to the front door, rang the bell and went in to see Kate and Taylor. After they had had a coffee and a brief chat, Taylor called Ben inside.

Emmy spoke with enthusiasm about Ben's bike riding skills, and heard that the three of them were planning a ride for that weekend in a nearby park. Ben seemed pleased at the thought of going to the park, but he was generally detached from the conversation. Emmy then asked about the recent afternoon at the lake. Taylor was able to get Ben interested in describing how the two of them had spent a good deal of time swimming underwater, searching for pretty stones. With a bit of enthusiasm, Ben went to his room and returned with five stones that he had collected that day.

In a casual, relaxed manner, Emmy wondered how hard it had been for Ben to come home after having such a good time. He looked confused, so she mentioned that Taylor had seen him banging his head against the tree. Ben immediately became angry with Taylor for telling Emmy about it. He said that it was not her business and that it didn't matter anyway.

Emmy quickly said, 'Oh, Ben, I'm sorry that you don't want me to know about it, but Taylor wanted to tell me because I'm your social worker and he thought that I might have some ideas about what it meant, and how to help you with whatever was going on for you. And he said that you hit your head so hard you were bleeding.'

Ben: Just a little bit, and I don't want to talk about it!

Emmy: You're not in trouble, Ben, I just need to understand why you did that.

Ben: I don't know!

Emmy: Let's figure it out, Ben, so we can find ways to help you not to do it again.

Ben: I won't do it again. Forget it.

Emmy: I can't, Ben. Were you angry with Kate and Taylor?

Ben: No, why would I be angry with them?

Emmy: I don't know, Ben, maybe you thought that they were being mean to you when they said it was time to leave the lake.

Ben: (*Shouting*) They're not mean to me!

Emmy: (*With some intensity, matching his emotional expression*) I'm glad, Ben, I was worried that something happened and that maybe...maybe you even thought that they didn't care for you as much as they used to.

Ben: (*Loudly*) You're stupid! They love me!

Emmy: I'm glad, Ben. I'm glad that you know that they love you. Then what's bothering you?

55

Ben: (*Still very loudly*) I DON'T WANT THEM TO LOVE ME!
          (*Suddenly Ben begins to cry and turns his back on everybody*)

Emmy: (*Her voice is now much quieter and gentler*) Oh, Ben, you
          don't want them to love you…and they do. You don't
          want them to love you…and they do.

          (*They all continue to sit around the table. Apart from Ben's
          sobs, it is quiet.*)

Kate: (*Very gently*): You can trust our love for you, Ben.

Ben: No, I can't! Sometimes I can tell how mad you are at
          me. You don't love me then. You say you do but you
          really don't!

Kate: But we do, Ben. We love you but we might be angry
          about something you do.

Ben: You have to say that! But I know you don't!

Kate: Oh, Ben, if you don't trust in our love for you, of course
          that would make it hard for you! I do understand that!
          I'm sorry that when we get angry at something you
          do sometimes, it makes you doubt whether or not we
          really love you.

Ben: I know you don't!

Kate: I'm sorry, Ben, that it feels that way to you.

Ben: I know I'm right.

Emmy: Ben is being very honest with us about what he believes,
          and it must be very hard for him to do that. Ben,

I wonder if you'd be able to tell us how this might help us to understand why you banged your head against the tree.

Ben: I said I didn't want to talk about it! (*Ben gets up and runs from the room. They hear him slam the door of his bedroom*).

Taylor: He doesn't want us to love him? What can we do?

Emmy: That must have been so hard for both of you to hear. Love is what he needs most in the world and he says he doesn't want it!

Taylor: He's been with us almost two years! When will he want our love?

Emmy: My guess, Taylor, is that right now he wants it and he doesn't want it. The part of him that doesn't want it is afraid of it. What if it won't last? What if you change your mind when you realise how bad he is? He thinks he doesn't deserve it and he believes that one day you will agree – he doesn't deserve your love.

Taylor: Should we not show our love for him?

Emmy: Probably it would be wise not to say too often that you love him, because that is likely to make him feel that he has to say that he loves you too. He needs to experience that you are committed to him – for better or for worse – and that you really enjoy doing things with him, you're interested in him and his interests, you're happy when he's happy. And when he says or acts as if he doesn't love you or want your love, accept what he is saying rather than getting angry or showing a lot of

57

distress when he is being so negative. And when you do get angry, bounce back fast, explain that your anger was connected to something he did, and ask him whether he'd like to talk about it or not, and then let it go.

Kate: I don't know if I can always be that way.

Emmy: Just like I think you need to accept Ben's negative feelings and attitudes, I think that you also need to accept your own negative feelings and reactions. Show him that the relationship is more important than what just happened, show that you're ready to repair it, accept his response, and then continue on. You don't have to be perfect, Kate. You have to show your commitment to the relationship. Admit it when you make a mistake, say you're sorry and have empathy for him if what you said, or did, caused him to be upset or not to trust you.

Kate: But what do we do when he's banging his head or hitting and scratching himself? Should we supervise him all the time so he can't hurt himself? Should we praise him when he seems upset but does not hurt himself? Should we scold him if he does hurt himself?

Emmy: You can't let his self-harming behaviour be the primary focus of your thinking about him. It cannot define who he is nor should the sole purpose of your relationship be to prevent it.

What to do? Before coming over today, I jotted down a few suggestions (*she hands Kate a piece of paper with a list*).

Emmy's advice

1. Be aware of his tendency to self-harm without being hypervigilant about it.

2. If he is self-harming, try to stop him gently and firmly, with empathy over the hard time he is having. Offer to help him but do not push it. He needs to choose wanting you to co-regulate his distress rather than trying to auto-regulate it with self-harming behaviour. You cannot force him to accept your support at those times, but you can keep offering it.

3. Be patient with the process; don't let him think that you feel it is hopeless. He's had years of self-doubt and a sense of worthlessness. It will take time for him to experience himself any differently.

4. If he initiates talking about it, be ready to listen with PACE.

5. If you agree, I will bring it up again when I come to visit next time. Discussing his self-harming behaviour cannot be avoided, nor should it dominate our conversation with him. We want him to think about it with us, not feel shame about it nor worry that we think he is bad or stupid when he hurts himself.

After Emmy left, Taylor prepared lunch while Kate did some work in the garden. Ben liked being in the garden and he soon joined her. They were able to have some light conversations, which carried over into lunch. The meeting with Emmy was acknowledged as having been hard, but then set aside as they focused on possible bike rides in the afternoon.

Over the next few days, Kate and Taylor followed Emmy's suggestion and did not initiate discussions about Ben's self-harming. And Ben definitely did not. Nor were there any conflicts or sources of stress that might evoke such behaviour. Daily life returned to "normal", and that meant that Kate and Taylor were still not confident that they understood their son very well. His inner life of thoughts, feelings and wishes remained concealed from them.

And then an event reminded them that their worries were not a thing of the past. What left them more confused and discouraged was that what happened can occur in all families and did not seem to be something that could be avoided. Taylor had surprised Ben the day before with a gift – a kit for assembling a model airplane – knowing that Ben was interested in planes and also enjoyed building things. Ben had been working on it for a few hours in his bedroom when Kate heard a scream and then a crashing sound. She ran to his room and saw pieces of the plane covering the floor and Ben in a corner with his back to her, grunting as he rocked himself. She went to him and saw that he had his arm in his mouth and was biting himself. She went to take his arm but he pulled away and continued to bite hard on it. She wrapped her own arms around him and pulled him towards her, and then placed her hands on his forehead and his arm. As he screamed at her to let go of him, he opened his mouth and she was able to pull his arm free. He pushed her away and crawled to the other side of the room, all the while shouting at her to leave. He did not put his arm in his mouth again, so she moved away from him and told him that she would just wait without bothering him until she knew that he'd be OK, before leaving the room. She sat watching him over the next 15 minutes as his breathing calmed and he seemed less agitated. She told him that she would leave him alone for a while, and that she'd be in the kitchen if he wanted her. She then left, but waited outside the door for a bit before going to the kitchen. Ten minutes later, she quietly checked up on him and he was lying on his bed, sleeping.

When Kate heard Ben stirring in his room an hour later, she invited him down for lunch, in a matter-of-fact way. She checked his arm, saw the bruising, and without asking, taped a large gauze patch over it, and commented that it would most likely be sore for a while. When Taylor came home a bit later, she did not comment on what had happened, and when Taylor asked Ben how the plane was coming along, she quickly said that Ben had been helping her in the garden most of the morning and hadn't had much time to work on it. Ben was quiet. Later, when they were alone, Kate told Taylor what had happened and they worried together.

Kate called Emmy to tell her, and they decided that they would try to start a conversation with Ben about it when Emmy visited the next day.

During the visit, Emmy asked Ben to show her what was growing in the garden, because Kate had invited her to pick and take whatever she wanted. Ben seemed proud of the garden, and when they went back into the house, he was quick to tell Kate what Emmy wanted.

He engaged easily in the general conversation. When Emmy expressed empathy for the trouble he had with building the plane, he didn't get angry but he became silent and put his head down. Emmy's voice remained gentle and soothing, focusing on how disappointing it is when something you really want to do does not work out as planned.

Emmy: What do you think bothered you the most when you couldn't build the plane the way you wanted to?

Ben: It was too hard! Dad, it was too hard!

Taylor: It was hard, Ben, I guess I didn't realise how hard it was.

Emmy: Was that what bothered you the most, Ben, how hard it was?

Ben: I thought Dad would be mad at me because I couldn't do it!

Taylor: Oh, Ben, no wonder you got so upset, you thought that I'd be angry with you for not being able to put it together. Now I understand why it bothered you so much! You thought I'd be angry with you.

(Taylor did not immediately reassure Ben that he was not angry. He first showed that he understood Ben's feelings and had empathy for him. This way of helping a child deal with a stressful experience is based on the attachment-focused training that was part of Taylor's adoption preparation. It helps the child to know that the parent really understands their experience. This is crucial if the child is to be able to accept the parent's support.)

Ben: I did think that you'd be angry, Dad. I wanted you to be happy that I liked your present and made the plane. Weren't you angry when Mum told you about it?

Taylor: No, son, I was not angry with you. I was sad for you because I knew that you really tried hard to build the plane and you were not able to do it the way you wanted. I knew how much you tried. And I was actually happy that you seemed to like the plane kit and that you tried so hard.

Ben: I did, Dad. And I'm sorry that I threw it when I couldn't make it and it broke! Now I can never put it together! Are you angry that I broke it?

Taylor: No, son, I'm not angry about that because I understand how upset you were that you couldn't do it. You tried so hard! And now I also understand how you were worried that I'd be angry with you. I'm not angry with you, son.

Emmy: You two do such a great job talking about what happened and what you both think and feel about it. One more thing, Ben. I wonder if you could tell us about what you were feeling when you bit your arm so hard.

Ben: I don't know why I did that. I just had to. Dad, are you angry with me that I bit myself?

Taylor: No, son, I'm not angry. I'm worried though when you hurt yourself. I don't want you to hurt yourself and I worry when you do. If you could tell us why you did it, maybe your mum and I and Emmy could help you to not hurt yourself.

Ben: I don't know why. But I just did. I couldn't stand it when
         I couldn't build it and then I couldn't stand it even more
         when I broke it.

Emmy: Maybe you were just so upset with it that the only
         way to show how upset you were was to bite yourself.
         Maybe because you were the most upset with yourself!

Ben: I guess. (*Ben is now quiet, pensive, becoming less engaged in
         the conversation and more focused on his own thoughts.*)

Emmy: Wow! This has been such a good conversation. And
         hard too! What do you think about it, Kate?

Kate: I agree with you, Emmy. Ben was so brave to be able to
         talk about it and he was able to help me and Taylor to
         understand why he was so upset and why he broke the
         plane and why he hurt himself. I'm glad that we had this
         conversation. (*Kate moves over and gives Ben a little hug.
         Taylor joins in.*)

Emmy: Well, family, there's not much more to say now,
         is there? I wonder if Ben will help me to pick the
         vegetables I'd like? And then I'll get home.

         When Ben and Emmy went outside, Kate and Taylor
         looked at each other with relief. They might have taken
         a step forward with Ben. He seemed to be able to face
         his challenges in a different way. No rage, no running
         to his room. After Emmy left, Taylor suggested to Ben
         that when they had the time, maybe they could drive to
         the game shop and buy another kit. They'd pick it out
         together and work on it together. Ben gave Taylor a hug
         and went to his room. They discovered later that he

had cleaned up his room so that they would not see the plane pieces all over the floor.

* * *

That was an important step for Ben, but there were many more to go. He continued to struggle with the challenges of his developing attachment to his adoptive parents. There were days when he would seem to be more relaxed and affectionate with them, but these times almost always led to him being more withdrawn and irritable afterwards. Kate and Taylor learned not to get too hopeful during the easy days nor too discouraged during the difficult ones. They realised that they needed to try to maintain an "even keel" in order to help Ben to stay more regulated. Both their excitement and distress made him more agitated and reactive.

About a month after the incident with the airplane kit, Ben was having an active day, riding his bike nearby, throwing a ball against the back of the house and building a mud dam over the stream that ran alongside their garden. Taylor called him to come in so that he would have time to clean the mud off his bike before dinner. Ben yelled that he needed to finish the dam first. Taylor saw that there was still quite a bit to do on the dam. He remained firm that Ben had to stop right there and then and get his bike cleaned. Ben swore at Taylor, and Taylor said firmly that he needed to stop swearing and come with him to the back of the house where the bike was. Ben shouted 'NO!' and began hitting himself in the face hard, again and again. Taylor ran to him, telling him to stop. Ben kept hitting himself and Taylor grabbed his arms. Ben tried to push Taylor away, but Taylor held him even closer while he thrashed around in his arms.

Ben kept saying 'No! Don't hold me!' Taylor said that
he would let him go if he agreed not to hit himself. Ben
kept yelling 'NO!' but then his anger turned to sadness
and he began to cry, still in Taylor's arms. Taylor held
him and rocked him gently. After a few minutes of
silence, Taylor told Ben that he could not let him hit
himself. Ben said that he had to hit himself. Taylor asked
him why, and Ben sobbed:

Ben: If I don't hit myself, I'll hit you and I don't want to hit
          you!

Taylor: You don't have to hit either one of us, Ben.

Ben: Yes, I do! And I don't want to hit you so I have to hit
          myself.

Taylor: Why do you think you have to hit one of us, Ben?

Ben: When I get mad, the only way to stop being mad is to
          hit someone. You made me mad and I wanted to hit
          you. The only way to stop myself from hitting you is to
          hit myself.

Taylor: I'm glad you don't want to hit me, Ben, but I'm sad that
          you hit yourself.

Ben: Don't be sad. It stops me from hitting you.

Taylor: Ben, may I show you other ways to handle your mad
          feelings toward me without hitting yourself? It's OK to
          be mad at me and to show me you are mad without
          hitting me. There are other ways, Ben, and I can teach
          you what they are. Will you let me teach you?

Ben: (*Looking into Taylor's eyes as if pleading with him.*) Yes, please teach me. Will you teach me?

Taylor: Yes, I will, Ben.

Ben: Teach me now, Dad, teach me now.

Taylor: I'll begin to teach you tomorrow, Ben. Mum has called us for dinner and I don't want us to be late.

Ben: But I haven't cleaned my bike, Dad.

Taylor: I'll help you with that after dinner. Would that be OK?

Ben: Yeah.

(*Taylor helps Ben up and puts his arm around him as they walk together to the kitchen door.*)

Later that evening, after Ben and Taylor had cleaned the bike and Ben had gone up to bed, Taylor told Kate what had happened. They were both sad, but cautiously hopeful. 'Another step', Kate said.

There were a number of steps in the weeks and months ahead, with Ben making new discoveries, learning to regulate new emotions and allowing himself to slowly develop a more comprehensive sense of self and others. Through his relationships with Kate and Taylor, his need to engage in self-harming behaviours gradually decreased, his intense negative affective states were co-regulated, and his ability to accept self-affirming experiences in his adoptive home gradually increased.

* * *

SECTION II

This case demonstrates four causes that are frequently present in children who self-harm:

- Anxiety in association with the positive experiences of self in the relationship with caregivers to whom they are forming an attachment. Ben's cry that he does not want Kate and Taylor to love him is an expression of his self-hate that drives him to avoid love, which, he fears, will only lead to abandonment.

- The need to punish themselves for their day-to-day failures, which reinforce the pervasive sense that they are inadequate.

- The need to direct their rage towards themselves when they are angry with their adoptive parents. The release of rage by self-harming behaviour is their way of staying regulated and redirecting their anger away from their adoptive parents.

- Self-harming behaviours are specific actions, which they are able to control, and when expressed, temporarily reduce their sense of hopelessness and helplessness.

Eddie only uses a few words: 'I don't know' and 'I don't care'

Stephen was trying to describe Eddie, aged 13, to Jen and Callie, foster carers who were interested in caring for her. He tried to help them to get a sense of the girl he was asking them to take into their home. He was not doing well.

'She really doesn't seek or want much attention', Stephen explained. 'She doesn't make many demands and seems to be content with most things that happen. It's not really clear why she has been asked to leave her other two foster homes. Her last foster carer said that Eddie just did not appreciate what they did for her. I can see why that might be frustrating at times, but it did not seem to be a serious enough problem to cause a carer to decide that a child has to leave after two-and-a-half years.'

'Did she complain a lot?' Callie asked, knowing that a constantly critical attitude could wear you down.

'I didn't hear that. Nor does she complain when I meet with her. She just doesn't seem to care that much about things. Like they don't matter to her.'

Jen wondered if Eddie was depressed.

'People have described her as being depressed. But she doesn't cry a lot or look sad. Sometimes I think that she's just not interested in talking to me. It doesn't seem to her to be that important whether I visit her or not.'

'Does she have friends?' Callie wondered.

'Her teachers say that she is on her own a lot, but not really isolated. She does talk with her peers but doesn't seem to have a best friend. Again, it's like she communicates that she wants to be left alone and so her peers do.'

'What does she say she wants in a foster home?'

'I asked her that and she said that she just wants to live with people who treat her fairly and are OK about her wanting a lot of time to herself. She says she likes to read and listen to music in her room. She doesn't like moving and says that she wants me to find a place where she can stay until she leaves school.'

'What does she want to do in her life?' Jen asked.

'She says that she wants to be a teacher and help kids to

learn how to be successful so that they can take care of themselves.'

'That's a nice goal to have', Callie said. 'In some ways, she seems to be saying that she wants to teach other kids what she has had to learn for herself.'

'How to be independent and not need anybody', Jen added.

Callie and Jen suggested that Stephen invite Eddie to spend the weekend at their house. Then the three of them could decide if it seemed to be the right placement for Eddie and they would let Stephen know on Monday.

Callie and Jen found Eddie to be pleasant and helpful during the few days she stayed with them. They told her what she might expect with regard to routines and privileges, and she said that was OK. She didn't have many questions for them.

Eddie's story

By the time they spoke with Stephen on Monday, Eddie had already told him that it was OK and she would like to live with them. Callie and Jen were a bit more enthusiastic about having Eddie move in with them. So she moved into her third foster home the following weekend.

Eddie became a foster child when she was six years old. She had been reported to Children's Services by her school. The teachers had described her as coming to school dirty and hungry most days when she attended, although she was often absent. She was a very quiet child but she did speak with a teaching assistant a little about her life. She talked about being left alone overnight, being forced to stay in her bedroom for hours at a time and being punished by not being allowed to eat. The subsequent child protection investigation revealed significant neglect, along with signs of substance misuse and domestic violence involving her parents.

Eddie's first placement lasted over four years. Her foster carers reported that she was not a problem and they had little to say about her daily life when the social worker visited. Eddie was quiet during the visits and never said anything to concern the social worker. It came as a surprise when the carers suddenly asked for Eddie to be moved as soon as possible. They described her as being "sneaky and needy". They said that she hoarded food, was destructive, and did not co-operate. They were not motivated to try to improve the placement, but communicated strongly that caring for Eddie had become a burden for them.

Eddie's second placement lasted two years. The foster carers were an older couple who found Eddie to be a 'good girl who doesn't cause problems'. They described her as being a quiet girl who spent a lot of time on her own, but they were not concerned about that, saying that 'Some people are just that way'. Unexpectedly, they decided that they did not want to continue as foster carers but to focus on their retirement instead. They asked Stephen if he could find another placement for Eddie at the end of the school year.

Eddie moves in with Callie and Jen

During the first few weeks of Eddie's placement with Callie and Jen, she seemed to "fit in" surprisingly well, with seemingly little effort. She was co-operative, polite and content. She initiated very little, to the extent that Callie and Jen didn't know what she liked or wanted to do. They joked that her two favorite responses were, 'I don't know' and 'I don't care'. After a while though, they began to worry about that. Why doesn't she know what she wants? Why doesn't she care what we do? If she seemed to be content with her life, shouldn't they be content too?

Once they began to wonder, it was difficult to stop. What if she really is not content? Maybe she is afraid to express what she wants. Maybe she worries that we will not like her if she disagrees with us. Maybe she is so vigilant about what she needs to do to please us that she gives little thought to her own wishes, feelings or ideas. Maybe what seems like contentment is her habitual need to attend to what is expected, what others want. Maybe she thinks that her ideas and wishes are not worth much. Maybe she thinks that she is not important. Maybe she assumes that no one – including us – is interested in her, or sees any value in who she is.

Jen and Callie arranged to speak with Stephen about their concerns, and after meeting with him, they were given an appointment to consult the agency's psychologist. They agreed on a way to reach out to Eddie that involved the following actions.

- Speaking to Eddie with PACE about her inner life whenever they were discussing external events and behaviours. Eddie needed to repeatedly experience acceptance and curiosity about her inner life rather than evaluations. She needed to experience empathy followed by reassurance. She needed to experience laughter and joy within the family, and to be encouraged to join in.

- The three of them taking turns in deciding what they would have for dinner, what games to play, where to go during free time. Eddie would be met with patience and playfulness if she had trouble making decisions; with empathy about not having had much experience in decision making.

- Callie and Jen modelling for her, in their own relationship, how to be mildly, but safely, frustrated by each other's differences, how to notice and accept each other's non-verbal communications, and how to repair their relationship after a conflict.

- Commenting with PACE whenever Eddie showed the slightest non-verbal expression of disappointment or frustration, and when appropriate, imagining what she might say to them if she used words to describe what she thought, felt or wanted.

- Assuring Eddie that it was not wrong to want to be alone in her room a good deal. However, she would also be encouraged to spend more time with the family. They would schedule family times if that made it easier for her. When she had chores, like washing the dishes, doing the laundry or weeding the garden, they would do them together; Jen or Callie would be casually chatting with her as they worked. These interactions would be casual invitations, not obligations. Eddie's quiet, withdrawn stance would still be accepted.

* * *

Over the next few weeks, Eddie often seemed anxious. No matter how lightly, and with acceptance, Callie and Jen reached out to invite her to participate and to be curious about her inner life, Eddie often seemed to convey a sense that she was afraid she might say or do something wrong. Being told that there was no right or wrong, simply thoughts and feelings and wishes, tended to make her uncertain, because if her thoughts and feelings and wishes were different from Jen's or Callie's, then she must be wrong. So whenever minor differences surfaced, Eddie would withdraw to her room. Jen and Callie completely accepted that. They realised that they were asking a lot of Eddie: to begin to relate to them differently than she had probably ever related to anyone in her life. She needed time on her own, to relax.

On one such occasion, Eddie had gone to her room to relax after the three of them had been weeding in the garden and played a friendly game of badminton. Jen went upstairs to ask her about dinner and Eddie's door was not completely closed. When she knocked, it opened wider, and she saw Eddie sitting on her bed. She had something in her hand and she looked startled.

Jen: I'm sorry, I didn't know the door would open when I knocked…What's wrong?

Eddie: Nothing. I'm not doing anything.

Jen: I'm not angry with you, Eddie, but I can tell that something is bothering you, what is it?

        (As Jen approaches the bed, she notices that Eddie has a needle in her hand.) Eddie, what are you doing with that needle?

Eddie: Nothing! I just found it outside.

        (Jen sits on the bed next to Eddie and takes the needle. Then she sees that Eddie's left arm looks like she has a rash. She takes her arm and looks closely to see a number of needle marks with small amounts of blood).

Jen: Eddie, you've been pricking your arm with that needle!

Eddie: I didn't mean to!

Jen: Eddie, I can tell those marks are not accidents. I know you must have done it on purpose.

Eddie: I'm sorry, I won't do it again.

Jen: Oh, Eddie, you've been hurting yourself with the needle. I'm sorry you felt that you needed to do that. I'm really sorry, Eddie.

Eddie: It didn't hurt much and I won't do it again.

Jen: I think it must have hurt, Eddie. And even if it only hurt you a little bit, I'm sad that you felt that you had to hurt yourself. Do you know why, Eddie? Why did you hurt yourself?

Eddie: I don't know. Sometimes I just feel I have to do it. So I do, and then I feel better.

Jen: Have you been doing it for long? (*Eddie nods.*)

Jen: When do you usually do it, Eddie?

Eddie: I don't know. I just do it. And after I do it, I don't need to do it again for a while.

Jen: Well, Eddie, I need to talk with Callie about what we can do.

Eddie: Am I going to have to leave?

Jen: No, I know we won't be telling you to leave. We just have to figure out how we can help you with this. We don't want you to have to feel that you need to hurt yourself.

Later Callie and Jen talked about how Eddie was hurting herself. They were sad and confused. They hadn't been aware of any signs that she was angry with them or with herself to give her cause to hurt herself. They had thought that she felt good about their efforts to make her more comfortable by doing things together with them. She did not talk much about what she thought or felt, but they had hoped that would come in time.

Jen worried because Eddie was hurting herself without any signs of being upset. 'It was just like she was combing her hair. It was strange that instead of being upset, her only worry seemed to be that she might have to move. It was like she was telling me about something that another child did. Like she observed it, not that she did it.'

Callie agreed that it was worrying, 'I guess we need to begin by talking with Stephen and see what he thinks. It really isn't something I was expecting. It would be easier knowing what to do if she had lied about it or was defiant like some of the other kids we've taken care of.'

Two days later they met with Stephen. He said that there had never been any reports of Eddie hurting herself when she lived in the other foster homes. Since Eddie said that she had been doing it for quite some time, Stephen assumed that her previous foster carers simply had not noticed. That was understandable, since they had left Eddie alone a lot because that was what she preferred. Stephen suggested that he speak with Eddie in a few days, to ask her about how she liked living with Callie and Jen in general, as well as exploring her self-harming behaviour.

When Stephen spoke with Eddie, she did not share anything new or distressing with him. He told Callie and Jen that she liked the placement and she had insisted that she didn't prick herself often, that the needle only just touched her skin and that it hardly hurt. When Stephen challenged her, Eddie stopped talking. Stephen suggested that he make a referral for Eddie to meet with a therapist in order to get an expert opinion about how serious the self-harming was, what it represented, and how best to respond if she did it again.

Over the next few weeks, while waiting to hear from a therapist, Callie and Jen stayed more aware of where Eddie was, what she was doing, and if it seemed like anything was troubling her. They noticed nothing unusual, other than that she seemed to be bothered by things less than other children they had cared for. It was also true that she showed fewer positive emotions. Most of the time, it was hard to know what Eddie was feeling. Then one day, Callie noticed that a small, but sharp, knife they used for cutting vegetables was missing. They asked Eddie if she had seen it and she denied having any knowledge of it. However, she seemed more tense than usual and they wondered if she had taken it. They watched her more closely in the following days.

One afternoon, Eddie came in from the garden and immediately went to her room. Jen sensed something was different about her, so a few minutes later she knocked on Eddie's door. When Eddie answered, Jen found Eddie sitting on her bed, looking guilty, as if she had done something wrong. Jen asked her what was happening and Eddie hung her head. Jen noticed that there was something under the blanket and she asked what it was. Then, as Jen watched, Eddie slowly put her hand under the blanket and pulled out the small, missing knife, leaving it on the bed. Jen sat next to her on the bed and took the knife.

Jen: Have you cut yourself with this?

Eddie: No.

Jen: Were you planning to?

Eddie: (after a period of silence) Yes.

Jen: Any particular thing bothering you that made you think of cutting yourself?

Eddie: No.

Jen: I've been wondering, Eddie, if you remember the first time you hurt yourself?

Eddie: Yes.

Jen: How old were you? Where were you living?

Eddie: I was living with Annie and Harry (*her birth parents*).

Jen: Did they used to hurt you?

Eddie: Yes.

Jen: What did they do?

Eddie: They always shouted at me and sometimes they slapped or punched me.

Jen: Both of them?

Eddie: Harry would hit me the most, Annie would shout the most and make me stay in my bedroom all day.

Jen: That must have been so hard, Eddie. Your parents hurt you instead of keeping you safe.

Eddie: Yes. (*No emotional expression.*)

Jen: Since they hurt you so often and so much, why do you think you also hurt yourself?

Eddie: I would just hurt myself a couple of times and then it didn't hurt any more and I felt better.

Jen: Did it feel better when Annie or Harry stopped hurting
         you?

Eddie: No, because I didn't know when they would hurt me
         again.

Jen: So if you hurt yourself, you knew that you could decide
         not to hurt yourself again, but you couldn't control
         whether Annie or Harry would hurt you again.

Eddie: Yes.

Jen: But hurting yourself did not make Annie or Harry hurt
         you less.

Eddie: Sometimes I thought it did. Sometimes I thought that if
         I hurt myself that day, they wouldn't hurt me till the
         next day.

Jen: And did that work?

Eddie: Sometimes.

Jen: So you thought that if you hurt yourself, your life would
         actually be better because it might make Annie and
         Harry hurt you less.

Eddie: Yes.

Jen: Do you think that's true here too, Eddie? Do you think
         that if you hurt yourself, it will be less likely that Callie
         or I will hurt you?

Eddie: You don't hurt me.

Jen: Do you think we would if you stopped hurting yourself?

Eddie: I don't know.

Jen: I promise you that we won't. (*Eddie does not respond.*)
          But maybe it's hard to feel sure about that.

Eddie: Yes.

Jen: Thank you for telling me about your hurting yourself,
          Eddie. And thank you for showing me the knife that I'll
          take back to the kitchen. (*Eddie does not say anything. Jen
          squeezes her hand for a moment and then leaves her room.*)

* * *

Over the next few weeks, Eddie seemed content and
comfortable living with Callie and Jen. But they were
not sure. Who was Eddie? She still seldom laughed,
became angry or seemed to be scared. They had not
yet seen her cry or get excited. But that slowly began to
change, and as Eddie became more expressive with them
emotionally, she spent less time in her room.

But one day they noticed welts on her arm. They
wondered if it was a rash, if perhaps she had rubbed up
against a plant and this was a reaction. Callie held her
arm and examined the welts more closely. Suddenly she
looked shocked:

Callie: Eddie, have you been pinching yourself?

Eddie: Yes.

Callie: Why, Eddie?

Eddie: I don't hurt myself so much when I do that and I thought you wouldn't mind.

Callie: We don't want you to hurt yourself at all, Eddie. Come into the kitchen with me, I'd like to wash it and to put some cream on the sore parts.

   (They go into the kitchen and Eddie sits while Callie gently cleans and rubs cream on her arm. As she finishes, she notices that Eddie has tears in her eyes. She leans over and strokes her hair, and Eddie begins to cry. Callie pulls her to her and hugs her.)

Callie: I'll take care of you. Whatever you need, whenever you want me to, I will take care of you. (*Eddie squeezes her tighter, not wanting to let go.*)

Eddie   (*after a few minutes, quietly*) I'm sorry I cried.

Callie: Why are you sorry?

Eddie: You'll think I'm a baby and I don't want to be a burden to you.

Callie: I feel happy that you are trusting me enough to cry. You're beginning to know how much I enjoy caring for you and how much I want to comfort you if you need to cry or if you're scared or sad.

Eddie: I'm afraid you'll change your mind.

Callie: You and Jen are my family. I will take care of you both when you need me to. So will Jen, she will take care of us both. We are family.

Eddie: I'm glad you're my family.

* * *

Over the next few months, Eddie became more and more spontaneous in sharing her feelings with Callie and Jen. She was louder – laughing and yelling – than they thought she could be. Callie and Jen became more spontaneous too. They were less cautious about saying or doing something that might upset Eddie. They were more confident that she would show or tell them if they upset her in some way. They also could sense what she was feeling more easily so they became more confident.

One day Eddie was quite angry with them for not letting her go out with another girl of her age whom they had not met before. She ran to her room. A few minutes later, Callie went up to see how she was doing.

Eddie: Why can't I go?

Callie: Because we don't know her. Have her visit us here first.

Eddie: I'm angry with you.

Callie: I know you are.

Eddie: It's your fault for not letting me go.

Callie: I don't think it's my fault or your fault. It just is because we are having a disagreement.

Eddie: You're not mad at me for being mad at you?

Callie: I am not mad at you for being angry with me.

Eddie: Is that part of being a family?

Callie: Yes.

Over dinner a few days later, Eddie said that she had something to tell them. When Callie and Jen looked at her, she said: 'I haven't hurt myself in 78 days.'

Jen: That's a long time.

Callie: Is that the longest time without hurting yourself since you came here?

Eddie: It's the longest time I can remember in the last 10 years since I began hurting myself.

Jen: Why do you think that is?

Eddie: I think it's because all this time I thought that hurting myself would make me feel better. Better than anything else I could do. Now I know I feel better by getting closer to you and telling you whatever I'm feeling.

(Callie and Jen just stare at Eddie, not knowing what to say. They each have tears in their eyes as they look at this courageous girl who has become their daughter.)

Eddie: What's the matter?? Why are you crying?

Callie: Because we're so happy that we're a family.

Jen: And that means you're our daughter.

* * *

As described in Section I, many children who have experienced considerable abuse and neglect when they were younger are not able to rely on new parents or carers for comfort and support. They attempt to regulate themselves – to soothe themselves – alone rather than by forming an attachment to their caregivers. Some of these children find that one way of taking some control over their life is through self-harm. They subject their body to a specific source of pain, and then they stop and the pain goes away and they feel better. What seems to the outsider to be self-harm is often motivated by an effort to self-comfort, and to self-regulate intense emotions. And they do feel better for a short time because the self-inflicted pain generates natural opioids in the body that do provide some comfort. Also, by focusing on the self-inflicted pain, they are able to distract themselves from the more chronic and unpredictable pain caused by abuse and neglect. Until these children are able to trust that their caregivers will comfort them and co-regulate their intense emotions, they may not be able to give up self-harming behaviours.

Because Eddie experienced severe neglect and abuse for a number of years, her sense of self was poorly developed and limited to experiencing herself as unlovable and bad. When she hurt herself, she actually felt more alive than she was usually able to feel. Because she was left alone to deal with her emotions, she tried to manage them by minimising, avoiding or denying them to a point where she habitually just did not feel anything. If she was not able to avoid her emotions, she tended to get some control over them through self-harm which she could direct and limit.

As Eddie gradually began to form a secure attachment to Callie and Jen, she also began to feel the emotions associated with a relationship with someone who noticed, enjoyed and comforted her. Developing such a relationship is most often a slow process for fostered and adopted children, with frequent pauses or efforts to flee from it. The training and support that Callie and Jen received from their social worker and fostering service was crucial for them to be able to be understanding and patient with the slow progress Eddie made in coming to trust them. Equally important was their being able to rely on each other for support.

SECTION II

References

Baylin J (2021) Personal communication

Baylin J and Hughes D (2016) *The Neurobiology of Attachment-Focused Therapy*, New York, NY: WW Norton

Golding K and Hughes D (2012) *Creating Loving Attachments: Parenting with PACE for Children with Attachment Difficulties*, London: Jessica Kingsley Publishers

Hughes D (2012) *Parenting a Child with Emotional and Behavioural Difficulties*, London: CoramBAAF

Hughes D (2016) *Parenting a Child who has Experienced Trauma*, London: CoramBAAF

Hughes D and Gurney-Smith B (2019) *The Little Book of Attachment*, New York, NY: WW Norton

Hughes DA, Golding KS and Hudson J (2019) *Healing Relational Trauma with Attachment-Focused Interventions: Dyadic Developmental Psychotherapy*, New York, NY: WW Norton

Hurley A (2021) *Parenting a Child with Difficulties in Learning Caused by Trauma*, London: CoramBAAF

CoramBAAF also publishes a pamphlet for foster carers that provides concise information on self-harm and how to help affected children – *Things Foster Carers Need to Know: Young people and self-harm* (Bond H, 2021)

Useful organisations

There are a number of organisations that offer support for people who self-harm, as well as their friends and families. We list a small selection here.

Alumina (previously Self-Harm UK)

A free online seven-week course for young people struggling with self-harm, to which they can refer themselves.

www.selfharm.co.uk

CAMHS (Child and Adolescent Mental Health Services)

An NHS service; details can be found on the NHS website.

Family Futures

Provides assessment and therapeutic support for children and their families.

Tel: 020 7354 4161

www.familyfutures.co.uk

Harmless

Provides support for self-harm and suicide prevention.

Email: info@harmless.org.uk

www.harmless.org.uk

Mental Health Foundation

Undertakes research and provides support around mental health.

www.mentalhealth.org.uk

www.mentalhealth.org.uk/a-to-z/s/self-harm

Mind

Provides support to those with mental health difficulties.

Tel: 0300 123 3393

Email: info@mind.org.uk

www.mind.org.uk

National Self Harm Network forums

Supports those who self-harm to reduce emotional distress.

https://wellbeinginfo.org/list/national-self-harm-network/

www.nshn.co.uk

PAC-UK (part of Family Action)

Provides specialist advice, support, therapy and counselling for all those involved in adoption and fostering.

Tel: 020 7284 0555

Email: advice@pac-uk.org

www.pac uk.org/

Samaritans

Provides support to anyone in emotional distress.
Tel: 116 123 (24 hours a day)
Email: jo@samaritans.org
www.samaritans.org

YoungMinds

Provides support to under-25s with mental health difficulties. The parents' helpline provides advice to all parents and carers.
Parents Helpline: 0808 802 5544 (9.30am–4pm weekdays)
YoungMinds Textline: Text YM to 85258
www.youngminds.org.uk